To T

A Journey Beyond Today

Dante' D. Barry

Copyright © 2024

All rights reserved.

To The Future

DEDICATION

To my mentors who have always prayed for me, covered me, and pushed me. Thank you.

To The Future

CONTENTS

1 Fear is not my future   6

2 Made for the future   16

3 Promoted for the future   26

4 Holy for the future   37

5 No more excuses   45

6 I can't come down   55

7 Prospering through prophecy   67

8 To the future and beyond   77

9 Im still on my way   88

To The Future

Introduction: A Journey Beyond Today

Life often feels like a series of intertwined moments—some joyous, some challenging—that shape our beliefs, our actions, and our hopes for the future. Each of us stands at the precipice of the unknown, navigating trials that test our faith, our resilience, and our vision. Yet, in the midst of uncertainty, one truth remains steadfast: there is a future waiting to be uncovered, one designed by the very hands of God.

This book is more than words on a page; it is a roadmap to propel you beyond your current reality. It is a guide to discovering the depth of God's promises, the strength of your identity in Him, and the power of a future rooted in His purpose. In these chapters, you will find inspiration, guidance, and prophetic truths that serve as both encouragement and challenge—a call to rise above limitations and embrace the destiny God has prepared for you.

Why This Book?
Throughout my journey, I have encountered seasons of pain, perseverance, and prophetic fulfillment. These experiences taught me that the battles we face are not without purpose. Every trial, every victory, every

moment of doubt was a thread woven into the tapestry of God's grand design. This book is birthed from that revelation—a message that declares boldly: your future is worth fighting for.

I wrote this book to remind you that no matter where you are today, you are not alone in the journey. The same God who called Moses out of the wilderness, the same God who led David from the fields to the throne, is the same God who is calling you into a future that surpasses your imagination.

What to Expect
This book is structured to take you on a journey of faith, transformation, and empowerment. Each chapter is intentionally crafted to address specific aspects of your walk with God, from

overcoming fears and embracing holiness to prospering through prophecy and standing firm against adversity. Together, these chapters weave a narrative that challenges you to leave behind excuses, distractions, and doubts, and step boldly into the future God has ordained.

We will explore stories from the Bible and real-life examples, unpacking truths that are as relevant today as they were thousands of years ago. You'll be encouraged to trust God's process, even when the path seems unclear, and to proclaim over your life that you are headed "to the future and beyond."

An Invitation

I invite you to read this book not just as a reader but as a participant. Allow the words to speak to your spirit, to ignite faith, and to stir up the courage needed to face what lies ahead. Take moments to reflect, to pray, and to declare over your life the promises of God. This is not just a book to be read; it is a call to action, a challenge to align your heart, your mind, and your actions with the future God has designed for you.

So, let's begin this journey together. Let's confront fears, tear down strongholds, and embrace the truth that we are made for more. As you turn the pages, may you find yourself inspired, uplifted, and emboldened to declare, "I am still on my way."

The future is calling. Will you answer?
— Dante D. Barry

Chapter 1: Fear Is Not My Future

Numbers 13:1-3, 17-33 (NIV), "Send some men to explore the land of Canaan, which I am giving to the Israelites. From each ancestral tribe, send one of its leaders."

Exploring the Promise

This simple directive from God was clear and full of promise. Yet, as the story unfolds, human fears and perceptions would complicate what should have been an act of faith. The men were sent to explore the land, taste its fruits, and witness its potential. However, their interpretation of what they saw revealed more about their inner fears than the actual conditions of the land.

When the spies returned, their report began positively: the land was as God had said—flowing with milk and honey, full of abundance. They even carried back the evidence: a cluster of grapes so large it required two men to carry it. However, their excitement quickly turned to doubt and fear. Ten of the spies gave a negative report, focusing on the size and strength of the people in the land:

"We seemed like grasshoppers in our own eyes, and we looked the same to them."

This statement revealed the root issue—not the giants in the land but the smallness of their faith.

Faith vs. Fear

In contrast, Caleb and Joshua stood firm in their belief that God's promise was greater than any obstacle. Caleb silenced the people, declaring:

"We should go up and take possession of the land, for we can certainly do it" (Numbers 13:30).

While Caleb and Joshua saw the promise through the lens of God's power, the others allowed fear to distort their perspective. Fear magnified their enemies and minimized their faith. It caused them to view themselves as defeated before the battle even began.

This pattern of fear is something many of us face. How often have we hesitated at the brink of a promise, not because the opportunity wasn't real, but because we doubted ourselves or God's ability to see us through?

The Transition from Moses to Joshua
By the time we reach **Joshua 1:1-9**, Moses has passed, and Joshua is commissioned as the new leader of Israel. God's instructions to Joshua are

filled with encouragement and commands to reject fear:

"Be strong and courageous. Do not be afraid; do not be discouraged, for the Lord your God will be with you wherever you go" (Joshua 1:9).

God knew the weight of Joshua's new role and the fear that could accompany stepping into Moses' shoes. Yet, He reminded Joshua—and us—that His presence is the key to victory. What Joshua lacked in experience or confidence, God would provide through His unwavering presence and power.

Divorcing Fear from the Future
As believers, we often wrestle with fear when facing the unknown. Fear whispers lies about our inadequacy,

distorts our perception of challenges, and keeps us stagnant. But the story of the Israelites reminds us that fear cannot coexist with faith if we are to walk into God's promises.

Faith requires action. Caleb and Joshua exemplified this by choosing to trust God's word over the intimidating realities before them. They saw the giants but focused on God's ability to overcome them. Their confidence wasn't in their own strength but in the One who had promised the land to them.

Identifying and Confronting Fear
Fear often disguises itself in our lives through excuses, hesitation, or over-analysis. It can appear as:

- A reluctance to forgive or reconcile, stemming from fear of vulnerability.
- Doubt about stepping into a new role or opportunity due to feelings of inadequacy.
- Clinging to old patterns because the unknown feels too risky.

But we must remember: fear is a liar. Its goal is to stagnate us, robbing us of the promises God has already declared as ours.

Walking into the Promise

God's promise is not theoretical—it is tangible and waiting for us. Yet, like the Israelites, we must choose to step into it with boldness. In Joshua's commissioning, God gave him clear instructions:

1. Be strong and courageous.
2. Meditate on His word day and night.
3. Obey His commands fully.

These principles remain true for us today. Success is not found in our abilities but in our obedience to God's word and reliance on His presence.

Fear Will Not Define You
2 Timothy 1:7 reminds us:

"For God has not given us a spirit of fear, but of power, love, and a sound mind."

This verse is a declaration of our identity in Christ. Fear has no authority in the life of a believer because God has equipped us with everything we need to overcome it.

A New Season of Faith

As we step into new opportunities and promises, let us leave fear behind. The giants in our path are no match for the God who goes before us. He has already secured our victory; we simply need to walk in it.

Isaiah 41:10-13 declares:
"So do not fear, for I am with you; do not be dismayed, for I am your God. I will strengthen you and help you; I will uphold you with my righteous right hand."

Fear is not your future. Instead, your future is one of faith, boldness, and the fulfillment of God's promises. The choice is ours: Will we let fear grip us, or will we grip fear by the neck and step boldly into the land God has prepared for us?

Today, let us declare: Fear is not my future.

Chapter 2: Made for the Future

Genesis 12:1-3 (NKJV)

"Now the Lord had said to Abram: 'Get out of your country, from your family and from your father's house, to a land that I will show you. I will make you a great nation; I will bless you and make your name great; and you shall be a blessing. I will bless those who bless you, and I will curse him who curses you; and in you all the families of the earth shall be blessed.'"

What if everything you're experiencing today is a setup for tomorrow? What if your trials, your growth, your victories, and even your failures are pieces of a divine plan designed to prepare you for a future you cannot yet see? These were the questions I reflected on when reading about Abram's journey. His call from God wasn't merely about the land he was leaving behind—it was about the generations that would be impacted because of his obedience.

Abram's journey reveals a critical truth: God doesn't always show us the full picture. Instead, He asks us to trust Him, step out in faith, and embrace the process of being "made." The call to "go" isn't always accompanied by clarity, but it is a call to preparation—a call to trust the One who knows the end from the beginning.

Being Made for the Future
Being made for the future implies readiness for what lies ahead. But in God's design, "ready" doesn't mean perfect. "Prepared" doesn't mean finished. "Good" doesn't mean complete.

Take Adam, for example. God declared His creation "very good," yet later said it was "not good" for man to be alone. This tells us that there's always room for growth and improvement, even in what seems complete. In the same way, every challenge, every test, and every season of life shapes us into what we need to become for the future God has planned.

Your current season is proof of this. Who you are today is a product of the lessons, challenges, and victories of yesterday. And just as the past prepared you for today, today is shaping you for tomorrow. It's an ongoing process, a continual molding by God's hands to make you into the person He's called you to be.

Overcoming Inadequacy
One of the greatest challenges in being made for the future is battling feelings of inadequacy. You may feel unprepared or uncertain, questioning whether you're truly capable of stepping into the future God has for you. But let me encourage you: inadequacy is not a disqualification—it's an invitation to depend on God.

Moses was 80 years old when God called him to lead Israel out of Egypt. Mary, the mother of Jesus, was a young teenager when she received the call to bear the Savior of the world. Their stories teach us that God isn't looking for perfection; He's looking for obedience.

Feeling unqualified or unready is actually a good sign. It means you're not relying on your own strength, but on God's power. When Peter stepped out of the boat to walk on water, he didn't wait to feel ready—he acted in faith. And it was that faith, not his ability, that enabled him to do the impossible.

Nations Are Calling

Abram's obedience wasn't just about him—it was about the nations that would come from him. God promised Abram that his descendants would be as numerous as the stars in the sky, and through him, all families of the earth would be blessed. But this promise required Abram to leave the familiar and step into the unknown.

In the same way, your obedience today isn't just about you. It's about the people you're called to impact—the "nations" waiting on the other side of your yes. These nations may not be literal countries but rather the people, families, and communities that will benefit from your obedience to God.

When you say yes to God, you are paving the way for others. Your children, your friends, and even people you may never meet will be impacted by the seeds you plant today. Just as Abram's decision to follow God set the stage for the coming of Christ, your obedience has ripple effects that reach far beyond your lifetime.

Lessons from the Journey
1. **Leaving the Familiar**
   Being made for the future requires leaving what's comfortable. Just as Abram had to leave his country and his father's house, you may need to step away from old habits, mindsets, or relationships that no longer align with where God is taking you. Growth often requires discomfort, but it's in the discomfort that transformation happens.

2. **Trusting the Process**
God's promises often come with a process. Abram didn't immediately see the fulfillment of God's promise, but he trusted God's timing. Similarly, we must trust that every step of the process—whether it feels good or not—is shaping us for what's ahead.

3. **Embracing Obedience**
Obedience isn't always easy, but it's necessary. When God calls us, He doesn't reveal every detail because He wants us to walk by faith. The key is to focus on what God has said, not on what He hasn't revealed.

Protection and Prosperity

As you step into the future, remember that God's promise includes both protection and prosperity. Genesis 12:3 assures us that God will bless those who bless us and curse those who curse us. This means we don't have to worry about defending ourselves or making things happen on our own. God is our defender and provider.

Prosperity isn't just about financial blessings—it's about thriving in every area of life. It's about having peace, purpose, and provision in abundance. When you align yourself with God's plan, you walk in His favor, and that favor impacts everything you touch.

Made for This Moment

You were made for the future, but the future isn't just a distant reality—it starts now. Every decision you make, every act of obedience, and every step of faith is shaping the future God has prepared for you. Don't let fear or inadequacy hold you back. You are enough, not because of your own strength, but because of the One who made you.

So as you engage the future, hold onto this truth: God is with you, and His plans for you are good. You were made for this moment, for this season, and for the future He has in store. Step forward with faith, knowing that the best is yet to come.

Chapter 3: Promoted for the Future

Genesis 50:20: *"You intended to harm me, but God intended it all for good. He brought me to this position so I could save the lives of many people."*

This powerful scripture encapsulates the profound truth that everything we endure has purpose. In the story of Joseph, the pain, betrayal, and trials were not obstacles; they were pathways. Joseph's journey from the pit to the palace was not just about his personal elevation but about the preservation of a nation. Similarly, your journey—the challenges, the setbacks, and even the betrayals—has prepared you for the position God intends for you to hold. You were promoted for the future.

Pain with Purpose

Promotion doesn't always feel like promotion. More often than not, it feels like pain. It disguises itself in hardships, trials, and losses that seem overwhelming. But in hindsight, every painful moment was a stepping stone, every challenge a test to refine your character, and every betrayal a tool to redirect your path. Joseph's own brothers betrayed him, selling him into slavery. Yet, in the end, he could say, *"You intended to harm me, but God intended it all for good."*

What if every painful experience in your life is God's tool to mold you, shape you, and prepare you for a role that only you can fulfill? The same people who betray you, the situations that stretch you, and the storms that challenge you are the vehicles God uses to position you for His purpose. Joseph's brothers couldn't see it, but their actions propelled him closer to destiny. Likewise, what others mean for harm, God uses to advance His plan for your life.

Promotion with a Mission

Divine promotion comes with responsibility. It's not just about elevating you for your benefit; it's about aligning you with God's greater plan to bless others. When Joseph was promoted to second-in-command over Egypt, it wasn't so he could bask in luxury. It was so he could save lives—those of his family and countless others.

In your promotion, there is a mission. The future isn't just about you; it's about the lives connected to your obedience, faithfulness, and perseverance. The gifts and anointing God has placed on you are not for your glory but to bring others closer to Him. Divine promotion aligns your personal growth with a corporate purpose. It ensures that your life is a conduit for God's blessings to others.

The Journey to Promotion
The journey to promotion often feels like a fight. Joseph's path was marked by opposition: sold into slavery, falsely accused, imprisoned, and forgotten. Yet, through it all, God was orchestrating events to bring him to his appointed position. Promotion doesn't come without opposition. The greater the call, the greater the resistance.

The enemy fights what he fears. If you've been under relentless attack—mentally, emotionally, financially, or spiritually—it's a sign that what's coming is greater than what you're facing. The enemy knows that if you reach your destiny, the ripple effect of your obedience will devastate his plans and bless countless others. Every trial is evidence of the future God is calling you to.

Maintaining the Integrity of Promotion

Joseph could have used his position for revenge. His brothers, who sold him into slavery, now stood before him desperate for help. Instead of repaying their betrayal with harm, Joseph chose forgiveness. Why? Because his promotion wasn't about them; it was about God. He understood that God had brought him to his position, not for personal vindication but for the salvation of many lives.

This is a critical lesson for anyone walking in divine promotion. With power comes the temptation to act out of pain, pride, or vengeance. But God's promotions are given to glorify Him, not to satisfy our human desires. Maintaining integrity in promotion means staying true to God's purpose, even when it means blessing those who hurt us.

Divine Promotion Requires Alignment

Divine promotion isn't about qualifications, degrees, or earthly accolades. It's about alignment with God's will. Before Joseph ever sat on the throne, God had already ordained him for that position. His promotion wasn't based on his abilities but on God's sovereignty.

God's plan supersedes human understanding. He orchestrates every detail—your upbringing, your experiences, even your pain—to prepare you for your role in His story. Jeremiah 1:5 says, *"Before I formed you in the womb, I knew you; before you were born, I set you apart."* This truth reminds us that promotion is not random; it is intentional. God has been preparing you for this moment your entire life.

Living for the Future
To fully embrace divine promotion, you must shift your focus from personal gain to God's glory. Promotion is not the end goal; it's a means to fulfill

God's purposes on Earth. The future depends on your obedience today. There are people, nations, and generations tied to your faithfulness.

Joseph understood this. His promotion wasn't about personal comfort but about saving lives. He told his brothers, *"God brought me to this position so I could save the lives of many people."* Likewise, your promotion is about the lives you will impact, the people you will serve, and the legacy you will leave.

Key Lessons from Joseph's Journey
1. **Opposition Precedes Promotion**
   The journey to promotion is often filled with challenges. These obstacles are not meant to destroy

you but to refine you for your destiny.

2. **Promotion Has a Purpose**
   Your elevation is not about you. It's about advancing God's kingdom and saving lives.

3. **God's Plan Over Your Plan**
   Divine promotion requires surrendering your desires to God's will. His plan is greater than anything you could imagine.

4. **Integrity Sustains Promotion**
   How you handle promotion matters. Responding to adversity with forgiveness and humility ensures that your promotion glorifies God.

5. **The Future Depends on You**
   Your obedience today sets the stage for God's work tomorrow. The lives connected to your destiny are waiting for you to step into your role.

Everything you have endured—the pain, the trials, the betrayals—was preparation. You were promoted for the future, not just for personal gain but for God's glory. Your position has purpose. Your future has meaning. And your obedience will change lives. Like Joseph, you may not understand it now, but one day you will look back and see that every step, every tear, and every trial was leading you to this moment.

You were promoted for the future.

Chapter 4: Holy for the Future

1 Thessalonians 5:23-24 (NLT)
"Now may the God of peace make you holy in every way, and may your whole spirit and soul and body be kept blameless until our Lord Jesus Christ comes again. God will make this happen, for he who calls you is faithful."

Called to Holiness

Living holy is a divine mandate for every believer, not just for the present but also for the future. Holiness is not about perfection; it's about submission. It is God who makes us holy, shaping us through experiences, relationships, lessons, and challenges. This sanctification process prepares us for His purposes, enabling us to reflect His nature, represent His character, and reveal His glory on earth.

Holiness Defined

Biblically, holiness means being set apart, consecrated, and dedicated to God. It is about living pure and undefiled, distinct from the culture around us. Holiness starts internally, transforming the heart and soul, and then finds expression in our actions and decisions. It is not achieved by human effort but through surrender to the work of the Holy Spirit.

The Process of Sanctification
When we accept Jesus Christ, we are imputed with righteousness—a position of holiness we did not earn. Yet, this is just the beginning. Like a parent learning to raise their child or an athlete mastering their craft, we grow into the holiness we have been called to. This process, known as sanctification, involves:

1. **Acknowledging our Position:** We are made holy by God through Christ. Holiness is a gift, not something we earn.

2. **Yielding to the Holy Spirit:** As we surrender daily, the Holy Spirit transforms our hearts and minds, making us more like Christ.

3. **Living Out Our Calling:** Holiness is not just a position; it's a lifestyle. It's reflected in how we talk, treat others, and navigate life's challenges.

Challenges to Holiness

Holiness can seem daunting, especially when faced with common struggles:

1. **Doubt:** Many feel unworthy or incapable of living holy lives.

2. **Lack of Confidence:** The fear of failure can paralyze believers.

3. **Few Examples:** A scarcity of role models makes it difficult to envision what holiness looks like.

However, holiness is not about perfection but being perfected. We are works in progress, continually being shaped by God's grace.

Key Insights for Living Holy

1. **It Starts with God:** Holiness is God's responsibility, but our role is to yield.

"Now may the God of peace make you holy in every way…" (1 Thess. 5:23).

2. **It's Possible to Be Kept:** Through trust and surrender, we can live lives that honor God.

"May your whole spirit, soul, and body be kept blameless…"

3. **It Requires Daily Surrender:** Holiness is developed through consistent submission to God's will.

"My old self has been crucified with Christ. It is no longer I who live, but Christ lives in me." (Gal. 2:20).

The Purpose of Holiness

Holiness is not for personal gain but for God's glory and the benefit of others. It positions us to:

- Reflect God's nature.
- Represent Him faithfully.
- Reproduce His character in others.

Our lives become a living testimony, showing the world who God is through our actions and decisions.

Holiness in Action

Practical steps to living holy include:

1. **Trusting in God's Work:** Recognize that He is faithful to complete the work He began in you. (Phil. 1:6).

2. **Following Godly Examples:** Learn from those who walk in holiness. (Heb. 13:7).

3. **Making Daily Choices:** Choose righteousness in every decision, big or small.

4. **Partnering with the Holy Spirit:** Allow Him to guide, correct, and transform you. (2 Cor. 7:1).

Holiness for the Future

Holiness prepares us for what lies ahead, ensuring we are equipped to handle the challenges and blessings of the future. It's about aligning our character with God's will so that we can fulfill our purpose and bring glory to His name.

As Ecclesiastes 12:13 states, *"Fear God and obey his commands, for this is everyone's duty."*

Let this be our ultimate goal: to live lives that are holy, pleasing, and wholly devoted to Him.

Chapter 5:
No More Excuses

Jeremiah 1:1–12 (NLT)
"These are the words of Jeremiah, son of Hilkiah, one of the priests from the town of Anathoth in the land of Benjamin. The Lord first gave messages to Jeremiah during the thirteenth year of the reign of Josiah, son of Amon, king of Judah. The Lord's messages continued throughout the reign of King Jehoiakim, Josiah's son, until the eleventh year of the reign of King Zedekiah, another of Josiah's sons. In August of that eleventh year, the people of Jerusalem were taken away as

captives. The Lord gave me this message: "I knew you before I formed you in your mother's womb. Before you were born, I set you apart and appointed you as my prophet to the nations." "O Sovereign Lord," I said, "I can't speak for you! I'm too young!" The Lord replied, "Don't say, 'I'm too young,' for you must go wherever I send you and say whatever I tell you. And don't be afraid of the people, for I will be with you and will protect you. I, the Lord, have spoken!" Then the Lord reached out and touched my mouth and said, "Look, I have put my words in your mouth! Today I appoint you to stand up against nations and kingdoms. Some you must uproot and tear down, destroy and overthrow. Others you must build up and plant."

In this passage, Jeremiah's encounter with God illustrates the gravity of divine calling and the excuses we often make to resist it. His immediate response to God's commissioning was to focus on his limitations: "I'm too young" and "I can't speak." Yet God, in His sovereignty, refused to accept Jeremiah's excuses. He corrected him, equipped him, and touched his mouth, giving him the confidence to fulfill his purpose.

Excuses—however valid they may seem—are hindrances to destiny. They delay purpose, derail progress, and distract us from the future God has planned. If we are to embrace the future fully, we must lay down every excuse and take up the responsibility of obedience.

Excuses: The Stumbling Blocks of Purpose

Excuses often stem from fear, insecurity, or a misunderstanding of God's character. Jeremiah's excuse of being too young reflected his insecurity, but God didn't let him dwell there. Instead, He assured Jeremiah of His presence, provision, and protection. This interaction reveals a truth we must embrace: God equips whom He calls.

When God speaks, excuses reveal where we are spiritually. They expose our fears and insecurities, but they also provide an opportunity for growth. God's response to Jeremiah's excuses wasn't condemnation but correction. He addressed the root of the problem—Jeremiah's doubt—and provided the assurance needed to move forward.

Similarly, our excuses often mirror our doubts about God's ability to work through us. Yet, as Jeremiah learned, the responsibility isn't ours alone. God Himself will provide the resources, courage, and words we need.

Excuses also stagnate progress. They not only delay personal growth but hinder the collective purpose of the body of Christ. Each of us is a part of a greater whole, and our obedience—or lack thereof—affects others. As Jeremiah's story shows, our calling is not just about us; it's about the people and purposes God has assigned to us.

No More Excuses: Lessons from Jeremiah

1. **God's Call Comes with Divine Provision**

Jeremiah's calling came with the promise of provision: "I have put my words in your mouth" (Jeremiah 1:9). This wasn't just a task for Jeremiah to accomplish in his own strength. God Himself provided the words, authority, and protection Jeremiah needed. Similarly, when God calls us, He equips us. Our role is to obey, trusting that He will handle the details.

2. **Excuses Are Truths Misaligned with God's Reality**

Jeremiah's claim of being too young was factually true, but it wasn't a truth aligned with God's perspective. In God's reality, Jeremiah's youth was part of the plan. God chooses the unqualified so that His power is evident. When we align our perspective with God's, excuses lose their power.

3. **God Knows Us Intimately and Assigns Purpose Accordingly**
"I knew you before I formed you in your mother's womb" (Jeremiah 1:5). This profound statement reveals that our calling is not an afterthought but a deliberate decision by God. Every detail of our lives—our background, personality, and even perceived limitations—is part of His plan to fulfill His purposes through us.

4. **Excuses Reveal Fear of Failure, but God Offers Assurance**
Fear of failure often fuels our excuses. We hesitate to step into

our calling because we fear falling short. Yet God assures us, as He assured Jeremiah, that His presence is with us: "Don't be afraid of the people, for I will be with you and will protect you" (Jeremiah 1:8).

Moving Forward: The Cost of Excuses

Excuses are costly. They rob us of the opportunity to grow, delay the fulfillment of God's promises, and hinder those who are depending on our obedience. Imagine if Jeremiah had persisted in his excuses. The prophetic words that shaped nations and preserved God's people might never have been spoken. The same is true for us. When we make excuses, we leave gaps in God's story—chapters unwritten, assignments unfulfilled, and lives untouched.

To move forward, we must adopt the mindset Jeremiah eventually embraced: no more excuses. This means confronting our fears, silencing doubts, and choosing obedience even when the task seems impossible.

The Future Awaits

The future God has planned is within reach. It is not a distant reality but something we are stepping into every day. However, to fully embrace it, we must let go of excuses. Whether it's fear, insecurity, or perceived limitations, we must trust that God's provision and power are enough.

Jeremiah's life teaches us that obedience unlocks the future. Despite his initial excuses, Jeremiah became a prophet who faithfully delivered God's word for over 40 years. His obedience, despite hardship and opposition, ensured that God's purposes were fulfilled through him.

Today, the same God who called Jeremiah is calling us. He is speaking over our lives, saying, "I knew you, I equipped you, and I sent you." The question is, will we respond with excuses, or will we say yes?

The future is waiting, and it depends on the excuses we refuse to make. No more excuses—only obedience.

Chapter 6: I Can't Come Down

Nehemiah 6:3 declares: *"So I sent messengers to them, saying, 'I am doing a great work, so that I cannot come down. Why should the work cease while I leave it and go down to you?'"*

This profound declaration by Nehemiah is not only a historical reflection of his resolve to rebuild Jerusalem's walls but also a spiritual mandate for believers today.

When God calls you to a task, distractions, opposition, and temptations will undoubtedly arise. These challenges are not just obstacles; they are opportunities to demonstrate your commitment to the work God has given you. Nehemiah's response—firm, clear, and resolute—serves as a timeless reminder: the work is too important, the future is too valuable, and the call of God is too weighty to allow anything to pull us down.

A Burden Becomes a Mission

The story of Nehemiah begins with a burden. The walls of Jerusalem lay in ruins, symbolizing the vulnerability and shame of God's people. When Nehemiah heard this, he was deeply moved—not by his own ambitions, but by the heart of God. He understood that the restoration of the walls was not just a physical task but a spiritual act that would reestablish the strength and dignity of God's people.

Nehemiah's burden propelled him into action. It wasn't enough to feel something; he had to do something. Often, the burdens we carry—the ones that keep us up at night, the issues that frustrate or irritate us—are not random. They are signals from God, pointing us toward our purpose. What breaks your heart may very well be the work God is calling you to repair.

Staying on the Wall: The Cost of Commitment

Building a wall wasn't glamorous. It was tedious, exhausting, and dangerous work. Nehemiah faced opposition from external enemies and internal dissent. Yet, in the face of all this, he declared, *"I cannot come down."*

Coming down implies abandoning the progress you've made. Every step forward in life—whether in your faith, family, career, or ministry—requires effort. You've fought battles, overcome obstacles, and climbed to new heights. Why would you risk undoing all that work by giving in to distractions?

Distractions come in many forms: fear, doubt, criticism, or even well-meaning voices urging you to take a break. But Nehemiah's response shows us how to stay focused. He understood that the future depended on the work being completed. If he came down, the wall wouldn't just remain unfinished; the entire city would remain vulnerable.

Lessons from Nehemiah's Resolve
1. **Recognize the Work as Great**
    Nehemiah described his task as a "great work." Recognizing the importance of what you're building changes your perspective. Whether it's your family, business, or ministry, when you see it as significant to God's plan, you'll guard it fiercely.
    Ask yourself: What has God called

you to build? A family founded on love and righteousness? A business that glorifies Him? A ministry that transforms lives? Whatever it is, declare over it, *"I am doing a great work, and I cannot come down."*

2. **Understand the Stakes**
   Nehemiah's work wasn't just about a wall; it was about securing the future of an entire nation. Your obedience today directly impacts the future—for yourself, your family, and generations to come. The enemy's attacks are proof of the significance of your work. If your effort didn't matter, there would be no opposition.

3. **Guard Against Distractions**
   Distractions don't always come in

the form of obvious threats. Sometimes, they're subtle— disguised as opportunities, relationships, or comforts that seem good but aren't God's best. Nehemiah faced distractions from people who appeared helpful but had ulterior motives. He discerned their intentions and refused to engage, saying, *"Why should the work cease while I leave it and go down to you?"*

4. **Stay the Course Despite Opposition**
Opposition is inevitable when you're walking in purpose. Nehemiah's enemies mocked him, threatened him, and spread lies. Yet, he refused to be intimidated. He prayed, strategized, and

continued building. His example teaches us to rely on God's strength and wisdom to overcome challenges.

The Wall as a Metaphor for Life

In Nehemiah's time, the wall symbolized protection, identity, and strength. Today, the "wall" represents the purpose, vision, and calling God has placed in your life. Building your wall means establishing something that glorifies God, protects what's valuable, and prepares for the future.

But just as in Nehemiah's time, the enemy seeks to breach the wall. His tactics haven't changed: he attacks the foundation, distracts the builders, and sows doubt. Your job is to stay on the wall, recognizing that the future depends on your faithfulness.

The Cost of Coming Down
Coming down from the wall has consequences. It means:

- **Tapping out:** Abandoning the work God has entrusted to you.
- **Negating purpose:** Allowing distractions to derail you from God's original plan.
- **Forfeiting the blessing:** The blessing is attached to the completion of the work, not just the beginning.

Like Nehemiah, you must declare, *"I will not come down."* You've come too far, fought too hard, and climbed too high to quit now.

Practical Application

1. **Focus on What Matters**
   Identify the "great work" God has called you to. Keep your focus on the task and refuse to let distractions steal your attention.

2. **Stay Rooted in Prayer and Action**
   Nehemiah balanced prayer with work. He sought God's guidance but didn't neglect the practical steps required to complete the wall. Faith without works is dead.

3. **Prepare for Opposition**
   Understand that challenges are part of the journey. Stay committed, knowing that God has equipped you to overcome.

4. **Build with the Future in Mind**
   Your work is not just for you. It's for the generations that will come after you. Build a legacy that glorifies God and blesses others.

Nehemiah's story is a powerful reminder of the importance of staying on the wall. Your faithfulness to the work God has called you to will impact not only your life but the lives of countless others. When distractions come, remember Nehemiah's words: *"I am doing a great work, so that I cannot come down."*

Declare over your life today: *"I will not come down. I am building something that matters. The future depends on it, and God is with me. I will complete the work."*

To The Future

The wall must be built. The future depends on it. Stay the course, and watch God's glory manifest through your life. **You cannot come down.**

Chapter 7: Prospering Through Prophecy

Ezra 6:14 declares, *"So the elders of the Jews built and prospered through the prophesying of Haggai the prophet and Zechariah the son of Iddo. And they built and finished it, according to the command of the God of Israel, and according to the decree of Cyrus, Darius, and Artaxerxes king of Persia."*

The Scripture illustrates a profound truth: prosperity is deeply connected to the acceptance, application, and obedience to the Word of God delivered through His assigned voices. This chapter delves into how God prospers His people, not just materially but holistically—spiritually, emotionally, and relationally—through His Word and guidance.

Understanding True Prosperity

In contemporary culture, prosperity often conjures images of material wealth—luxury cars, sprawling mansions, and overflowing bank accounts. While material blessings can be a part of God's provision, the biblical concept of prosperity is far more encompassing. To prosper in God is to thrive in every area of life: soul, mind, relationships, health, and purpose.

God's plan for prosperity is always purposeful. It aligns with His story, His kingdom, and His glory. Prosperity is not an end in itself but a means to advance God's work on earth.

The Balance of Suffering and Prosperity

An essential part of understanding prosperity is recognizing its counterpart: suffering.

Romans 8:17 reminds us, *"If we are children, then we are heirs—heirs of God and co-heirs with Christ, if indeed we share in His sufferings in order that we may also share in His glory."* Suffering and prosperity work together, each revealing different facets of God's character and plan.

In the life of Joseph, we see a vivid picture of this balance. Sold into slavery, falsely accused, and imprisoned, Joseph faced immense suffering. Yet, even in his lowest moments, Genesis 39:23 tells us, *"The Lord was with Joseph and gave him success in whatever he did."* Prosperity and suffering intertwined, preparing Joseph for a greater purpose: to save nations in famine.

Similarly, our prosperity in God often emerges through the refining fires of suffering. Both are tools in His hands, shaping us and revealing His glory.

Prospering Through the Word

The elders of the Jews prospered not through their efforts alone but through the prophesying of Haggai and Zechariah—prophets assigned to guide them. God's Word, when spoken, received, and applied, releases prosperity in every area of life. This prosperity transcends circumstances, as Divine favor locates and blesses His people regardless of their environment.

Consider the Hebrew word for "prosper" in Ezra 6:14, *matsliach*, which means "to make progress, thrive, or flourish." Prosperity in God is not limited to a single dimension of life. It is holistic, ensuring success and progress even in challenging seasons.

The Role of Assigned Voices

Throughout Scripture, God assigns specific voices to guide and prosper His people.

In Hosea 12:13, it is written, *"By a prophet, the Lord brought Israel out of Egypt, and by a prophet, he was preserved."* Prophetic voices are God's instruments for direction, correction, and blessing.

However, prospering through prophecy requires a posture of humility and submission. It necessitates:

1. **Acceptance** – Receiving the Word as truth, as Paul describes in 1 Thessalonians 2:13: *"When you received the word of God which you heard from us, you accepted it not as*

the word of men, but as it actually is, the word of God, which is indeed at work in you who believe."

2. **Allowance** – Letting the Word take root and transform your life, as Colossians 3:16 exhorts: *"Let the message of Christ dwell among you richly."*

3. **Application** – Putting the Word into practice. Jesus states in Matthew 7:24, *"Everyone who hears these words of mine and puts them into practice is like a wise man who built his house on the rock."*

Only when we accept, allow, and apply the Word can we unlock the full benefits of God's prosperity.

The Covenant of Prosperity

As heirs of Abraham through faith in Christ (Galatians 3:7-9), we inherit the blessings promised to him. God declared to Abraham in Genesis 12:2-3, *"I will bless you and make your name great, and you will be a blessing. I will bless those who bless you, and whoever curses you I will curse; and all peoples on earth will be blessed through you."*

This covenant ensures that prosperity is not just for personal gain but for the blessing and advancement of others. 2 Corinthians 9:11 reinforces this, stating, *"You will be enriched in every way so that you can be generous on every occasion, and through us your generosity will result in thanksgiving to God."*

Key Insights on Prosperity

1. **Starting and Finishing** – God prospers what is actively being built for His glory. Ezra 6:14 highlights that the elders of the Jews prospered as they built. Prosperity requires action—faith coupled with works.

2. **The Role of the Word** – Prosperity is directly tied to the Word of God spoken through assigned voices. It is our responsibility to receive and act on that Word.

3. **For His Glory** – God prospers us not just for our benefit but to advance His kingdom. His authority supersedes all earthly powers, ensuring His plans prevail.

Living in True Prosperity

Prospering through prophecy is about aligning ourselves with God's Word and His purposes. It is not about chasing material wealth but embracing a life that reflects His glory in every area. True prosperity flows from obedience, trust, and a heart postured toward Him.

As we build what God has commanded, He promises to bless the work of our hands. Let us commit to starting, continuing, and finishing the assignments He has given us, knowing that His plans for us are good—to prosper us and give us a future filled with hope. **Let's prosper His way.**

Chapter 8: To the Future and Beyond

Ephesians 3:20 (NKJV)
"Now to Him who is able to do exceedingly abundantly above all that we ask or think, according to the power that works in us."

A God Beyond Our Imagination

God is not limited by human understanding, expectations, or efforts. He is a God who exceeds every hope, dream, or prayer we can imagine. The promise of *Ephesians 3:20* assures us that our future in Christ is not just a continuation of our plans but an invitation into a reality far beyond what we could conceive. This chapter explores what it means to trust God fully, letting His power at work in us lead us to a future that reflects His glory, not our limitations.

Faith: The Foundation of Our Future

The battle for the future begins with where we place our faith. Faith is the currency of the kingdom, the bridge between our present reality and God's extraordinary plans. If we place our faith in human effort, possessions, or fleeting gratifications, the results will reflect the limitations of those investments. However, when our faith is rooted in God, the outcomes are infinite, exceeding anything we could dream of.

God's ability to do exceedingly abundantly is tied to the power working in us. This power—Christ in us—shapes our future as we yield to Him. Our surrender activates His plans, which often look very different from what we might have envisioned.

The Context of Ephesians 3:20

In his letter to the Ephesians, Apostle Paul emphasizes the eternal role of the Church and its purpose within God's divine plan. The first three chapters lay out the Church's identity and mission, while the last three chapters focus on how believers should live to fulfill God's purpose. Paul highlights the unity, maturity, and faith required to experience God's abundance. This context underscores a crucial truth: our individual lives are interwoven into a greater corporate purpose for God's glory.

God's Plans vs. Our Expectations

Often, God reveals just a glimpse of what He plans for our lives. Like King David, who was anointed as a young shepherd but faced years of trials before becoming king, we may not see the full picture. The promise is sure, but the process requires trust, patience, and faith.

We might dream of a future based on our desires and limited understanding, but God calls us to something far greater. His plans for us are rooted in His eternal wisdom and glory, not in our human limitations. When we focus on our inadequacies or try to achieve His promises through our own efforts, we risk missing the fullness of His purpose.

Beyond Human Strength

In the beloved movie *Toy Story*, Buzz Lightyear initially believed he was more than a toy. He declared, "To infinity and beyond!" with confidence in his own abilities, only to realize that his strength was limited. His journey teaches a profound lesson: to reach an unlimited future, we must rely on a power beyond ourselves.

Buzz's story mirrors our own struggles. We often try to achieve God's plans in our own strength, only to fall short. It is when we acknowledge our limitations and yield to God's power that we can truly soar to the future and beyond. His plans require our trust, not our control.

The Role of Surrender

God's power works in us as we surrender our will, emotions, and understanding to Him. Surrendering doesn't mean passivity; it means active trust in His sovereignty. It requires laying down our assumptions and leaning fully on His promises.

Proverbs 3:5-6 reminds us, "Trust in the Lord with all your heart, and lean not on your own understanding; in all your ways acknowledge Him, and He shall direct your paths." Trusting God takes us beyond what we can comprehend, propelling us into His supernatural possibilities.

God's Exceedingly Abundant Power
God's ability to do "exceedingly abundantly above all we ask or think" speaks to His nature as a generous and limitless Father. However, this promise is not automatic; it requires alignment with His will and surrender to His power.

1. **Exceedingly:** God surpasses our expectations. He goes beyond our prayers, dreams, and plans.

2. **Abundantly:** His blessings overflow, providing not just enough but more than enough.

3. **Above:** God lifts us beyond human possibilities into supernatural realities.

This abundance is not about material wealth alone. It encompasses joy, peace, purpose, and fulfillment that surpasses circumstances.

Freedom Through Truth

Our journey to the future often involves confronting lies we've believed about ourselves. These lies, rooted in past experiences, insecurities, or cultural pressures, can limit our faith and hinder God's work in us. Jesus reminds us in *John 8:32*, "You shall know the truth, and the truth shall make you free." True freedom comes from embracing God's truth about who we are and His plans for us.

The Divine Exchange

When we surrender our plans to God, He exchanges our limitations for His limitless power. This divine exchange is beautifully illustrated in *Romans 8:28*: "And we know that all things work together for good to those who love God, to those who are the called according to His purpose." Even our mistakes and trials become part of the tapestry of God's goodness, shaping us for His glory.

A Call to the Future

To move to the future and beyond, we must:

1. **Yield to God's Power:** Recognize that we cannot achieve His plans in our own strength.

2. **Trust His Timing:** Understand that delays are often part of His preparation process.

3. **Embrace His Promises:** Hold on to the truth that He is faithful to complete what He began.

Exceedingly, Abundantly, Above

The future God has prepared for us is not just the next chapter—it's an entirely new story. As we align ourselves with His will, surrendering our limitations and trusting in His power, we position ourselves to experience His exceeding, abundant, and above-all grace.

The journey to the future and beyond requires faith, not in ourselves but in the One who is able. As we yield to

Him, we will discover a life filled with His miraculous power, far beyond anything we could ask, think, or imagine.

Now to Him who is able to do exceedingly abundantly above all that we ask or think, according to the power that works in us, to Him be glory in the church by Christ Jesus to all generations, forever and ever. Amen. (Ephesians 3:20-21)

Chapter 9: I'm Still On My Way

Matthew 2:13-23 (NKJV)
"Now when they had departed, behold, an angel of the Lord appeared to Joseph in a dream, saying, 'Arise, take the young Child and His mother, flee to Egypt, and stay there until I bring you word; for Herod will seek the young Child to destroy Him.'"

Destined for a Purpose

The story of Jesus' early years reveals a profound truth about destiny: when God has marked you for a purpose, the enemy will go to great lengths to stop you. King Herod's attempt to destroy Jesus was not based on what Jesus had done but on the potential of who He would become. This chapter explores the realities of surviving attacks, overcoming obstacles, and pressing forward with the declaration, "I'm still on my way."

The Cost of Destiny

From the moment Jesus entered the world, He was a target. Herod's massacre of innocent children was a desperate attempt to eliminate a perceived threat to his throne. Similarly, the enemy often targets those with a significant purpose, attempting to derail them before they can realize their calling.

Your survival is not an accident. The battles you have faced—the loss, betrayal, hardship, and pain—are evidence of the greatness inside you. Like Jesus, you have been protected by God's hand, guided through trials, and prepared for a future that cannot be thwarted by the enemy.

Obstacles as Preparation

God often allows obstacles to shape and strengthen us for the journey ahead. Joseph, Mary, and Jesus' flight to Egypt symbolizes divine protection, but it also required obedience and trust in God's instructions. Each step—leaving their home, traveling to a foreign land, and waiting for God's timing—was a test of faith.

In the same way, your journey has not been without challenges. Yet, those challenges have been preparing you for what's next. As you obey God and trust His leading, you are being positioned for impact, even when the path seems unclear.

The Enemy Tried, but God Prevailed
Like Herod's failed attempt to destroy Jesus, the enemy's plans against your life have not succeeded. The fact that you are still here, still breathing, and still pressing forward is evidence of God's faithfulness.

"If God is for us, who can be against us?" (Romans 8:31).

The enemy may have tried to silence you with discouragement, distract you with fear, or derail you with setbacks, but God's purpose for your life remains intact. Every attack has only served to strengthen your resolve and refine your character.

God's Protection and Guidance
In Matthew 2, we see God's intentional protection over Jesus. Through Joseph's obedience to divine instructions, Jesus was shielded from Herod's schemes. The angel appeared not once, but three times, guiding Joseph to make decisions that ensured Jesus' safety.

This same divine guidance is at work in your life. Even when you are unaware, God is orchestrating your steps, placing you in environments that protect and prepare you. The relationships, opportunities, and even the closed doors are all part of His plan to guide you toward your destiny.

Lessons from Jesus' Journey

1. **Obedience Brings Protection:** Joseph's willingness to follow God's instructions saved his family. Your obedience, even in uncertainty, positions you for God's protection and provision.

2. **The Enemy's Plans Will Fail:** Herod's schemes were futile because God's purpose for Jesus was unstoppable. Similarly, no weapon formed against you will prosper (*Isaiah 54:17*).

3. **God's Timing Is Perfect:** Joseph waited for the angel's instruction before moving. Trusting God's timing, even when it feels slow, ensures you stay aligned with His will.

A Bold Declaration

As you reflect on the battles you've faced, declare with faith: *"I'm still on my way."* This declaration is not just a statement of survival but a proclamation of victory. It is a reminder that God's plans for you are still unfolding and that the enemy's attempts to stop you have failed.

Prophetic Insights

1. **Divine Guidance Leads to Safety:** Just as the angel guided Joseph, God is leading you to places of

safety and purpose. Be attentive to His voice and trust His direction.

2. **The Enemy Targets Impact:** The attacks on your life are not just about you but about the impact you are called to have. Your obedience and perseverance are crucial to fulfilling your purpose.

3. **Victory Is Guaranteed:** The assassination attempts on your destiny have been reversed. God has already defeated the enemy on your behalf.

Surviving to Thrive

Survival is not the end goal—it's the beginning of a much greater journey. Consider the story of Chris Gardner, as portrayed in *The Pursuit of Happyness*.

Gardner's life was marked by profound challenges: homelessness, financial despair, and the responsibility of caring for his young son. Yet, despite these adversities, he refused to let his circumstances define his destiny. Instead of succumbing to hopelessness, Gardner demonstrated extraordinary perseverance and faith.

In the movie, Gardner's journey is filled with moments of heartbreak and resilience. From sleeping in subway restrooms with his son to tirelessly pursuing a competitive internship at a brokerage firm, Gardner's story is a powerful testament to the determination it takes to rise above survival mode. He endured rejection after rejection, worked tirelessly during the day, and studied late into the night

―all while holding onto the vision of a better life for himself and his son.

Gardner's eventual success didn't come by chance; it was the result of his unyielding belief that hardship was temporary and that thriving was possible. His journey reminds us that survival is not the finish line. It is the fertile ground where faith, hard work, and vision take root.

Your struggles, like Gardner's, are birthing something greater. The sleepless nights, the tears, and the sacrifices you make today are all seeds being sown into a harvest of purpose, provision, and promise. As you declare, "I'm still on my way," you are prophesying over your life that your best days are ahead. Just as Gardner's story inspires us to believe in what's possible beyond the struggle, your journey will inspire others to keep going and never settle for merely surviving. You are called to thrive.

From Survival to Impact

Because you survived, you are now positioned to thrive. Every challenge, every setback, and every tear has been preparing you for the fulfillment of God's promises. Like Jesus, Moses, and countless others who faced opposition early in life, you are destined for greatness.

"And we know that all things work together for good to those who love God, to those who are the called according to His purpose." (Romans 8:28).

To The Future

Let this truth anchor your heart: you are still on your way. The road may not have been easy, but the journey is worth it. As you move forward, may you walk with confidence, knowing that God's plans for you are exceedingly, abundantly above all you could ask or think.

Declare it boldly: *"I'm still on my way."*

To The Future

About The Author

Danté D. Barry

Let's Connect

- Danté D. Barry
- @dantedbarry
- Kingdom Headquarters

Made in the USA
Columbia, SC
13 December 2024